D0997649

Junior
How to Draw
Cars, Trucks and Planes

Published by Top That! Publishing plc
Tide Mill Way, Woodbridge, Suffolk, IP12 1AP, UK
www.topthatpublishing.com
Copyright © 2011 Top That! Publishing plc
0 2 4 6 8 9 7 5 3 1
Printed and bound in China

Introduction

Have you always wanted to draw cars, trucks and planes, but were put off because they looked too difficult? Have no fear! This book shows you a fun and easy way to draw vehicles!

Just follow the tips and step-by-step instructions, and you'll soon learn a set of basic drawing techniques that you can then apply to any subject.

Top Tip!

To draw good, clean lines, you need to keep your pencils nice and sharp with a pencil sharpener.

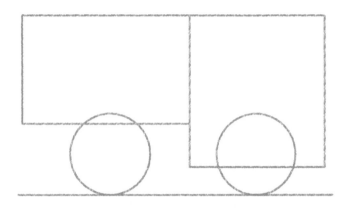

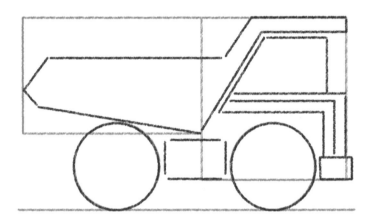

Basic Shapes

When you want to draw an object, a good way to start is to look at the object carefully and to break it down in your mind into a series of simple shapes — triangles, squares, rectangles, circles and ovals.

Notice which shapes are bigger or smaller than others, and where they join together. Look carefully at their angles and proportions. Spend time just looking before you pick up your pencil!

Tools of the Trade

You will need a pencil, an eraser, a pencil sharpener, a ruler, a fine black marker pen and fibre-tip pens or pencils for colouring in your drawings.

Four Simple Steps

You can apply the 'basic shapes' technique to drawing any subject, including cars, trucks and planes. You can use it for simple front-on and side-on views, as well as for more complicated angled views. All it takes is four simple steps ...

Construction lines

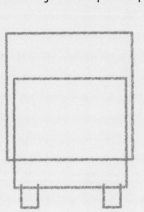
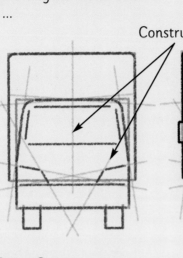

Step 1. First, break the vehicle down into basic shapes. Sketch them in pencil.

Step 2. Next, sketch construction lines to help you get the right angles, and draw a pencil outline.

Step 3. Build up the detail, then go over your pencil outline in pen.

Step 4. Rub out the guidelines and add colour to bring your picture to life.

Perspective

Many of the drawings in this book show objects seen from an angle. When you look at a drawing, it should be obvious where the artist was in relation to what they were drawing. This is known as 'perspective'.

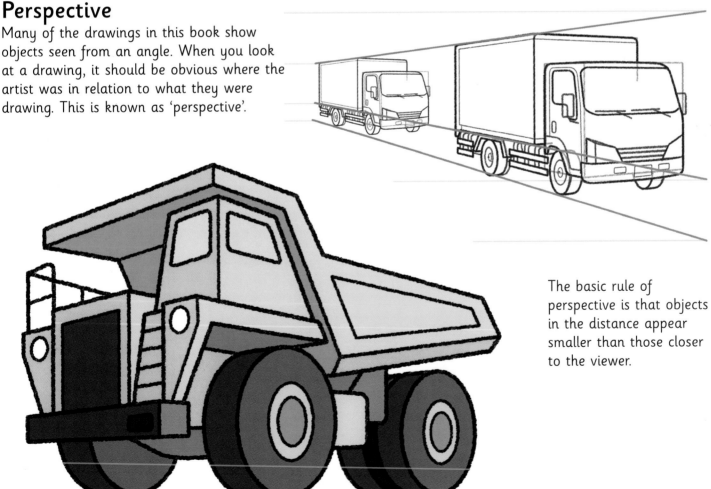

The basic rule of perspective is that objects in the distance appear smaller than those closer to the viewer.

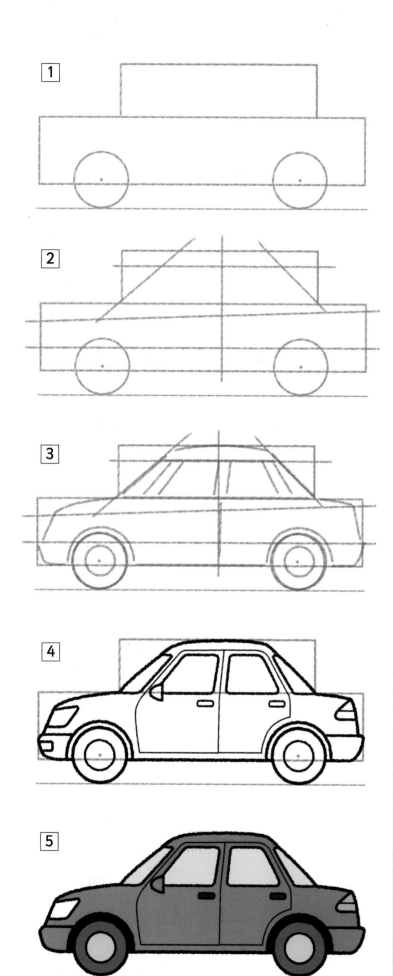

Car Side-on

Use these simple shapes to help you draw the side-on view of a car.

Step 1. First, with a pencil and ruler, lightly sketch a line for the road. Next, draw a long rectangle. Add two circles for wheels and a smaller rectangle on top of the first one, positioned just off-centre.

Step 2. Next, sketch construction lines to show the angles of the car. Draw them for the top and sides of the windows, the main body angles, and a vertical line where the doors meet.

Step 3. Now draw the outline of the car's body. Notice that the bonnet and boot slope downwards. Draw the window shapes, the wheel arches and two smaller circles inside the wheels.

Step 4. Go over your outline with a fine black marker pen. You can now rub out the pencil guidelines and start to draw in the finer details. Draw the lights, wing mirror, door handles and windscreen.

Step 5. Rub out any remaining pencil guidelines and colour in your car with fibre-tip pens or pencils.

Car Front-on

Now that you've mastered a car from the side, see if you can tackle one from the front!

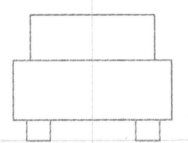

Step 1. Sketch two small squares for wheels and two rectangles for the body.

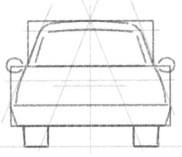

Step 2. Sketch a centre line and construction lines for the angles. Then draw the car's outline.

Step 3. Go over the outline in black pen and add detail – radiator, lights, mirrors.

Step 4. Rub out the pencil guidelines and finish your drawing by colouring it in.

Creating Different-shaped Cars

Use these basic shapes to create a small car, a sports car and an estate car. Look carefully to see how the shape and angles of each car are different.

Small Car

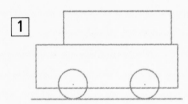

Step 1. For this car, draw the smaller rectangle right of centre.

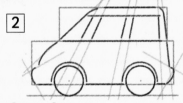

Step 2. Add construction lines to give you the angles of the body. Then draw the outline.

Step 3. Go over the outline in pen, add details and colour in.

Sports Car

Step 1. For a sports car, the two rectangles are centred.

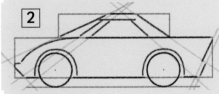

Step 2. Using construction lines, sketch the short roof, curved bonnet and slanting tail end.

Step 3. Outline in pen, add details and colour in brightly.

Estate Car

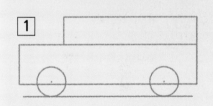

Step 1. For the estate car, line up the rectangles to the right.

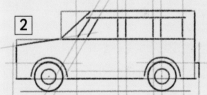

Step 2. Add construction lines to give you the angles of the sloping windscreen and bonnet.

Step 3. Go over your outline in pen, add details and colour in.

Other Cars to Try

Every car looks different. See if you can sketch these well-known cars using the techniques you have learnt.

Beetle Front-on

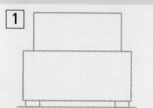

Step 1. Sketch these basic shapes. The middle rectangle is slightly taller than the top one.

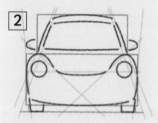

Step 2. Next, sketch in construction lines to give you the angles, then draw the outline.

Step 3. Add details and go over your outline in black pen.

Step 4. Rub out the guidelines and colour in your Beetle.

Beetle Side-on

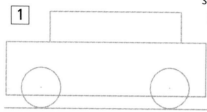

Step 1. Sketch the basic shapes for a side-on view of a car, plus a line for the road. Notice that the top rectangle is not quite central.

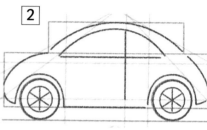

Step 2. Next, sketch construction lines and the car's curved outline. Add windows and wheels.

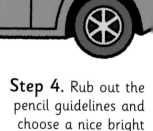

Step 3. Add further details, then go over your pencil outline in black pen.

Step 4. Rub out the pencil guidelines and choose a nice bright colour for your Beetle.

Mini Cooper Front-on

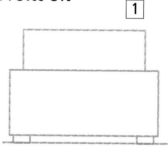

Step 1. First, sketch two small rectangles for wheels, then a large rectangle with a smaller one on top.

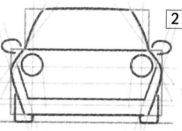

Step 2. Next, sketch construction lines to give you the angles of the car's body. Draw the outline, adding headlamps and wing-mirrors.

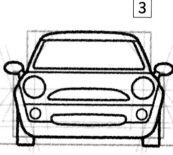

Step 3. Add the wide radiator, number plate and other details. Then go over your outline in pen.

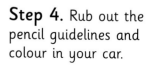

Step 4. Rub out the pencil guidelines and colour in your car.

Wrangler Jeep Front-on

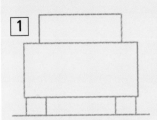

Step 1. Start with a line for the road. Then sketch two squares, wide apart, for wheels, topped by two rectangles.

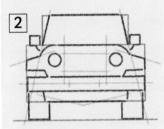

Step 2. Next, build up the outline using construction lines to give you the angles.

Step 3. Add details and go over your outline in black pen.

Step 4. Rub out the pencil guidelines and colour in your jeep.

Chevy Bel Air Front-on

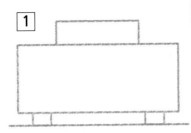

Step 1. First, sketch the basic shapes – two small squares for wheels, then a wide rectangle with a smaller one on top, positioned centrally.

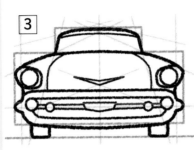

Step 3. Add further details, then go over your outline in black pen.

Fact File

The American Chevrolet Bel Air, with its hooded headlights and stylish tail fins, was a classic car of the 1950s. It has appeared in many films.

Step 2. Next, sketch construction lines to give you the angles for the body, which curves in and out. Draw the outline.

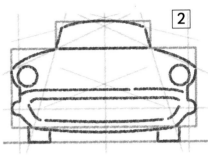

Step 4. Rub out the pencil guidelines and colour in your classic Chevy Bel Air.

Wrangler Jeep Side-on

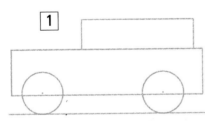

Step 1. Sketch a line for the road, two circles for wheels and a large rectangle, to the right of centre. Add a smaller rectangle on top, also to the right of centre.

Step 2. Next, build up the outline, giving a slight slant to the jeep's roof, bonnet and tail end.

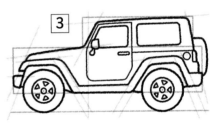

Step 3. Add details such as hubcaps (wheel covers). Then go over your outline in black pen.

Step 4. Rub out any pencil guidelines and colour in your jeep.

Try These Cars

The Porsche 911, the Pagani Zonda and the powerful F1 racing car are all built for speed, but are very different shapes.

Porsche 911

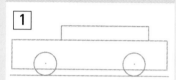

Step 1. Sketch a line for the road and two circles for wheels. Next add a long rectangle centred over the wheels. Then draw a small rectangle on top, to the right of centre.

Step 2. Draw the car's curved outline, with its long, sloping back. Add windows and wheels.

Step 3. Add the details shown here, and then go over your pencil sketch in black pen.

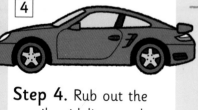

Step 4. Rub out the pencil guidelines and colour your Porsche in a bright, bold colour.

Pagani Zonda

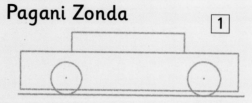

Step 1. Sketch a line for the road, two circles, a large rectangle close to the road and a small rectangle centred on top.

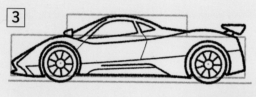

Step 4. Rub out any pencil lines and colour in your speedy supercar.

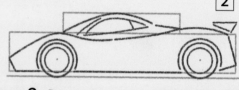

Step 2. Draw the car's outline. The body sweeps down under the window and curves up at the back, out of the box.

Step 3. Add details, including the triangular spoiler at the back that helps the car to grip the road. Go over your outline in black pen.

F1 Racing Car

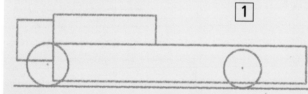

Step 2. Study the outline shape of the racing car and copy it into your guideline boxes.

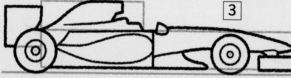

Step 1. Sketch a road line and two circles for wheels. Next, draw a long rectangle very close to the road line, far to the right of centre. Add a thin rectangle on top and an almost square rectangle at the tail end.

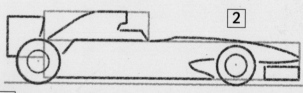

Step 3. Add more detail. Then go over your pencil sketch in pen.

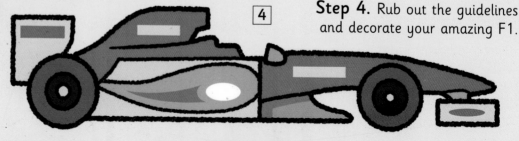

Step 4. Rub out the guidelines and decorate your amazing F1.

Stylish Sports Cars

Time to test out your drawing skills on these three fun, super-cool sports cars. Ready? Get set, go!

Fact File

Ferruccio Lamborghini, from Italy, started out building tractors. He went on to design stylish supercars made for long-distance travel.

Lamborghini Gallardo

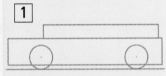

Step 1. Sketch a line for the road, two circles for wheels and a long rectangle slightly to the left of centre. Add a small rectangle on top, almost lining up with the right edge of the large rectangle.

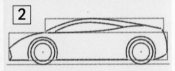

Step 2. Next, sketch the sleek outline shape of the car with its short, curved bonnet.

Step 3. Add the details shown here, and then go over your pencil outline in black pen.

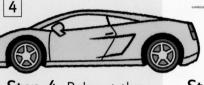

Step 4. Rub out the pencil guidelines and colour in your speedy, comfortable supercar.

Bugatti Veyron

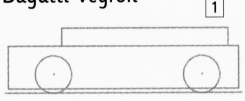

Step 1. Sketch the guideline shapes for the Bugatti Veyron. The large rectangle is slightly to the left of centre, and the small one is to the right.

Morgan Aero

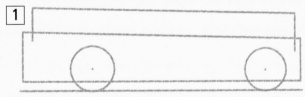

Step 2. Next, draw the car's outline and the sleek curve of the bodywork over the front wheel.

Step 4. Rub out the pencil guidelines and colour in your classic sports car.

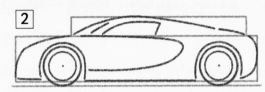

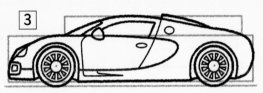

Step 2. Next, sketch the car's curved outline and add some details.

Step 3. Build up the detail, especially on the wheels. Then go over your outline in black pen.

Step 4. Rub out the guidelines and choose a smart colour for this very stylish car.

Step 1. Sketch a line for the road, two circles and a large rectangle slightly to the left of centre – make the right edge of the rectangle slightly shorter than the left edge. Add a long, thin rectangle on top.

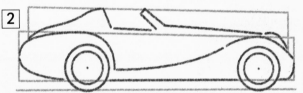

Step 3. Add detail, then go over your outline in black pen.

Car at an Angle

Here is the basic technique for drawing a car at an angle. Add your own construction lines to help you with the angles.

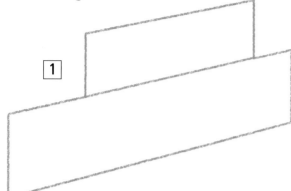

Step 1. Start by sketching a large, slanting rectangle (called a parallelogram). Then sketch another, smaller one on top.

Step 2. Next, draw two more boxes exactly the same as the first two, but slightly lower down and to the right.

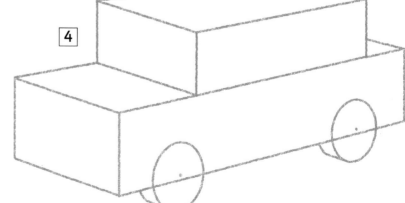

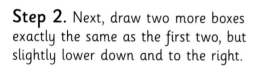

Step 3. To make your boxes look three-dimensional, join up the top and bottom of the two small boxes with four slanting lines, and the top and bottom of the two large boxes with another four slanting lines.

Step 4. Now your car is starting to take shape! Carefully rub out some of the pencil lines, as shown, and add the outlines of the wheels.

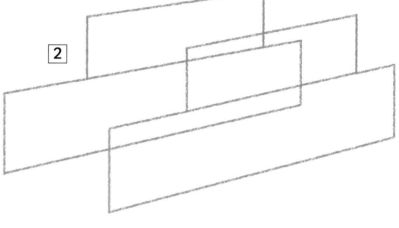

Step 5. Next, draw the 'side' of the car, fitting it into the guideline boxes, as shown.

5

6

Step 6. Continue to build up the car's body, adding in the front and roof. Use a ruler to help you keep both ends of each line an equal distance from the box edges.

Step 7. Once you are happy with the outline, rub out the ends of the pencil lines that you drew to get the angles right.

7

8

Step 8. Go over your sketch in black pen and add details such as doors, lights, radiator and bumpers.

9

Step 9. Finally, rub out any remaining pencil guidelines and colour in your drawing using pens or pencils.

Dump Truck

Have fun drawing this mighty dump truck.

Fact File

A dump truck has a huge engine. When the body of the truck tips up to unload, the weight of the engine stops the truck from tipping over backwards.

Front-on View

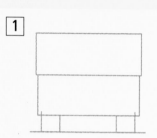

Step 1. First, sketch two small squares and two large rectangles.

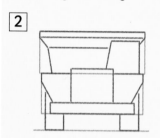

Step 2. Next, sketch the truck's outline into your guideline boxes.

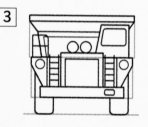

Step 3. Add lights and other details, and go over the sketch in pen.

Step 4. Complete your mighty truck by colouring it in!

Side-on View

Step 1. Using a pencil and ruler, sketch a road line, two circles and two rectangles, as above.

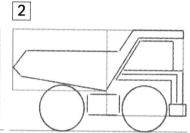

Step 2. Using the boxes as a position guide, sketch in the outline of the truck.

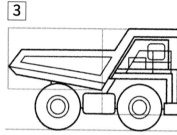

Step 3. Build up the details, then go over the pencil lines in black pen.

Step 4. Rub out the guidelines and complete your dump truck by colouring it in.

Angled View

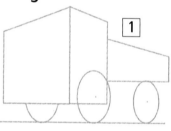

Step 1. Sketch the shapes above to create guideline boxes for an angled view of the truck.

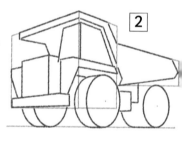

Step 2. Next, sketch the outline of the truck inside the boxes. Use the boxes as a guide to make sure your lines and angles are correct.

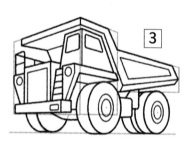

Step 3. Add further detail to your truck. Once you are happy with the outline, go over the pencil sketch in fine black pen.

Step 4. You can now rub out the pencil guidelines and bring the dump truck to life by colouring it in!

Bus

Try your hand at this bus. Then have fun colouring it in with pens or pencils.

Front-on View

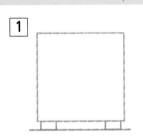

Step 1. Sketch this simple guideline box for a front-on view of a bus.

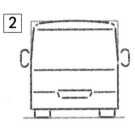

Step 2. Inside the box, sketch in details such as a curved roof and large windscreen.

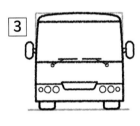

Step 3. Add further details such as lights, then go over your sketch in black pen.

Step 4. Rub out the guidelines and colour in!

Side-on View

Step 1. Using a pencil and ruler, sketch a rectangle and two small circles.

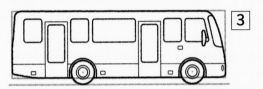

Step 3. Build up the detail until you are happy with your sketch. Then carefully go over the pencil lines in black pen.

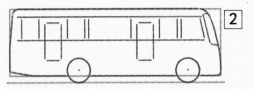

Step 2. Inside your guideline box, draw the outline of the bus, adding windows and doors.

Step 4. Finally, rub out the pencil guidelines and colour in your bus. You could add passengers, too!

Angled View

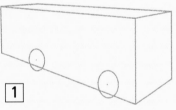

Step 1. First, draw a three-dimensional shape using slanting rectangles. Add two circles to show where the wheels will go.

Step 2. Next, sketch the outline of the bus inside your guideline box. Include doors and windows, and add wheel arches.

Step 3. Build up the detail and add markings. Once you are happy with your sketch, go over the pencil lines in black pen.

Step 4. Rub out any remaining pencil lines, then choose a smart colour scheme for your bus and colour it in.

Truck

Put your drawing skills to the test by having a go at this powerful truck.

Fact File

Trucks have large, powerful engines, which they use to pull weights of more than 10 tonnes.

Side-on View

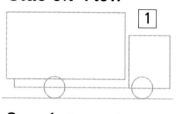

Step 1. For a side-on view, use a ruler and pencil to sketch these guidelines.

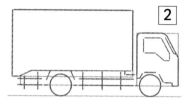

Step 2. Next, draw the shape of the truck and guidelines for the side bars.

Step 3. Build up the details in pencil, adding lights, mirror, side bars and wheel hubs. Then go over your pencil lines in black pen.

Step 4. Rub out any pencil lines and colour in your truck. Why not add a smart company logo?

Front-on View

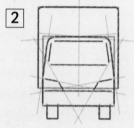

Step 1. For your guidelines, draw four squares, as shown.

Step 2. Next, draw the truck's outline inside your guideline boxes.

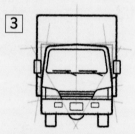

Step 3. Build up the details, then go over the pencil lines in black pen.

Step 4. Rub out the pencil guidelines and colour in your truck.

Angled View

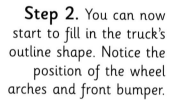

Step 1. Using a pencil and ruler, sketch these guideline shapes. Try and copy the angles of the sloping lines shown here.

Step 2. You can now start to fill in the truck's outline shape. Notice the position of the wheel arches and front bumper.

Step 3. Sketch in more details and then go over your pencil outline in black pen.

Step 4. Rub out any remaining pencil lines and colour in your truck. Include dark shadows around the side bars and tyres.

Fire Engine

Look out! Here comes an exciting red fire engine to draw.

Front-on View

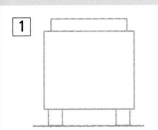

Step 1. Sketch a set of guideline boxes using these shapes.

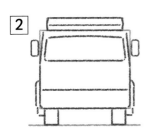

Step 2. Fill in the outline of the fire engine.

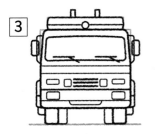

Step 3. Carefully add lots of detail, then go over your pencil lines in black pen.

Step 4. Colour your engine bright red!

Side-on View

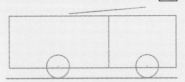 [1]

Step 1. First, sketch two guideline boxes, two circles for wheels, and a line for the ladder.

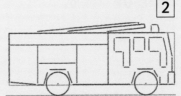 [2]

Step 2. Next, draw the outline of your engine and add details – ladder, lights, windows and wheel arches.

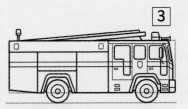 [3]

Step 3. Build up the details and draw in the central stripe. Then go over your pencil lines in black pen.

[4]

Step 4. Rub out any remaining guidelines and colour your engine in bright red, to make it easily recognisable.

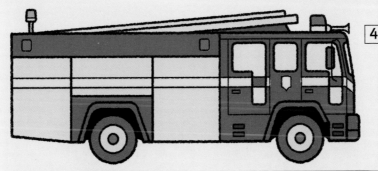

Angled View

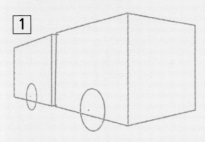 [1]

[2] **Step 2.** Next, draw the engine's outline and begin to add detail and definition. Include windows and, on top, a siren, a long light and the ladder.

Step 1. To create a three-dimensional guideline box, sketch a slanting rectangle split into two, a slanting square and two circles for wheels.

[3]

Step 3. Build up more detail, then go over the pencil lines in black pen.

Step 4. Rub out the guidelines and colour in. Some engines have a yellow stripe to make them stand out at night.

 [4]

Cement Mixer

The trickiest bit of a cement mixer to draw is the cone-shaped mixer itself.

Fact File

A cement mixer keeps turning all the time to stop the cement inside it from going solid too soon.

Front-on View

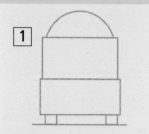

Step 1. Sketch this guideline shape for your cement mixer.

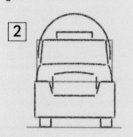

Step 2. Draw the outline, using the top box for both the windscreen and bonnet.

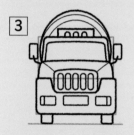

Step 3. Add lights, mirrors and radiator bars, then go over your pencil lines in pen.

Step 4. Colour in your mighty mixer!

Side-on View

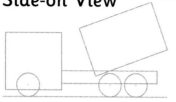 **1**

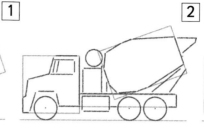 **2**

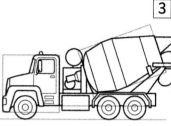 **3**

Step 1. Start by sketching three circles, then a square and two rectangles. These are the guideline shapes for your cement mixer.

Step 2. Next, outline the driver's cab and the mixer, which is roughly the shape of an ice-cream cone.

Step 3. Add details to the mixer, as shown here. Once you are happy with your drawing, go over the pencil lines in pen.

4

Step 4. Rub out any remaining guidelines and colour in your cement mixer with pens or pencils.

Angled View

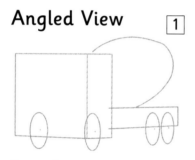 **1**

Step 2. Next, copy the outline shown here into your guideline boxes. The three-dimensional wheels soon make the drawing take shape.

2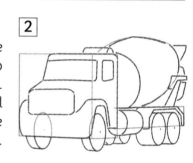

Step 1. Lightly sketch these basic shapes to represent the driver's cab, the mixer and the wheels. Notice that the wheels are ovals, not circles.

3

Step 3. Add further details until you are happy, then go over your pencil lines in black pen.

4

Step 4. Rub out any remaining pencil guidelines and colour in your mixer in bright, bold colours.

Monster Truck

Have fun drawing this monster racing truck!

Fact File

Bob Chandler was the first person to build a monster truck, in the 1970s. He named it Bigfoot!

Front-on View

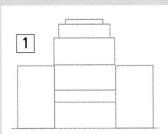

Step 1. Sketch eight rectangles to create the basic shape of the truck.

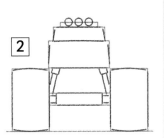

Step 2. Curve the edges of the body and wheels. Add suspension bars and lights.

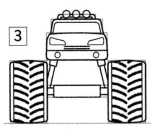

Step 3. Draw the tyre treads and other details, then go over in pen.

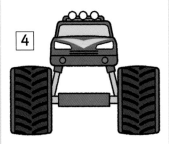

Step 4. Rub out the guidelines and colour in your monster truck.

Side-on View

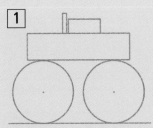

Step 1. Sketch two large circles and a rectangle, then add two smaller rectangles on top.

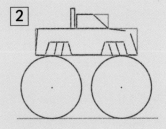

Step 2. Draw the truck's outline inside the boxes.

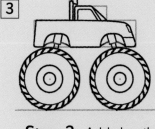

Step 3. Add details to your monster truck, including tyre treads, lights and windows. Then go over your outline in black pen.

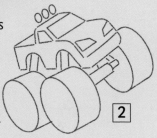

Step 4. Rub out any pencil guidelines and colour in your mighty monster.

Angled View

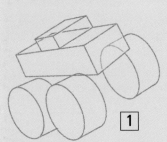

Step 1. Start by lightly sketching three cylinders for the wheels and two boxes for the truck's body. Take your time to work out the angles.

Step 2. Draw the truck's curved outline inside the guide boxes. Then carefully rub out the straight lines of the boxes. Pencil in lights, windows and suspension bars.

Step 3. Pencil in further details such as tyre treads and any markings you may want to include. Once you are happy with the sketch, go over it in black pen.

Step 4. Finally, rub out any remaining pencil lines, and colour in and decorate your monster racer.

Aeroplane

Now that you've mastered land vehicles, try your hand at some fantastic aeroplanes!

Fact File

The Wright brothers built the first successful aeroplane and made the first controlled human flight on December 17th, 1903.

Side-on View

Step 1. First, sketch a long rectangle, two smaller rectangles to represent the wheels, another rectangle for the cockpit and a square for the plane's tail.

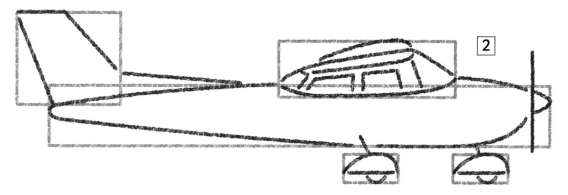

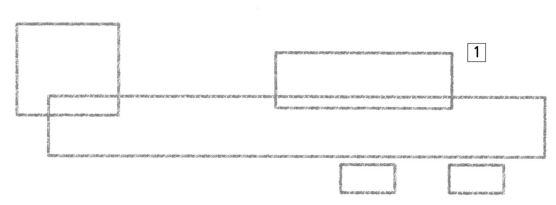

Step 2. Using your boxes as guidelines, draw a side-on view of the plane. Include its wheels, propeller, tail fin, cockpit and wings (on top of the cockpit).

Step 3. Add more details such as doors, handles and tail parts. Once you are happy with the drawing, go over it in black pen.

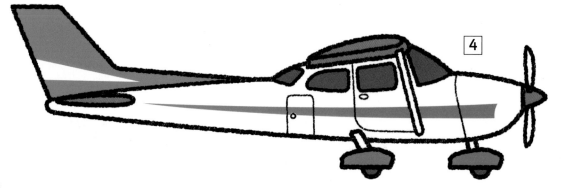

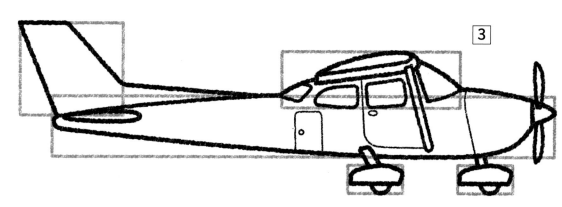

Step 4. Rub out the guideline boxes and colour in your plane using pens or pencils. Don't be afraid to highlight parts or add some markings.

Flying High!

Make your plane soar with these underneath and above views!

Top Tip!

Experiment with different paper and pencils to find favourites that work best for you.

Underneath View

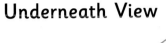

Step 1. First, sketch two three-dimensional boxes for the plane's body. Then add the shapes shown here for the tail and wings.

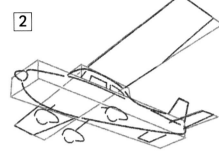

Step 2. Next, carefully copy the outline of the plane into your guideline boxes.

Step 3. Continue adding details until you are happy with your picture. Then go over your pencil lines in black pen.

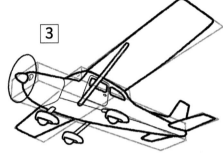

Step 4. Rub out any remaining guidelines. Now bring your aeroplane to life by colouring it in. Have fun with the colours!

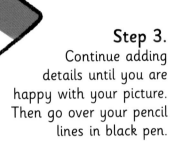

Above View

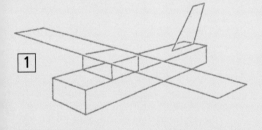

Step 1. Create your guideline boxes as shown above. Try to get the angles right, and keep your lines straight with a ruler.

Step 2. Sketch the plane's curved outline inside the boxes, and begin to add details such as wheels, windows and propeller.

Step 3. Add wing supports, propeller blades and any other details. Then go over your pencil outline in black pen.

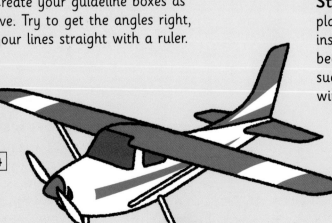

Step 4. Rub out the pencil guidelines and give your plane some colourful markings. You could always add a runway, too!

Spitfire
The famous Spitfire is great to draw!

Fact File
The Spitfire was a British single-seater fighter plane used throughout World War Two.

Angled View

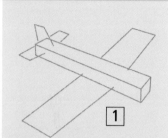

Step 1. Create your guideline boxes, as shown above.

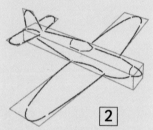

Step 2. Draw the plane's outline, with its wide, curved wings.

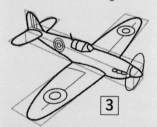

Step 3. Add details and markings. Then go over your pencil lines in black pen.

Step 4. Rub out the guidelines and have fun adding the Spitfire's distinctive colours.

Front-on View

Step 1. To create the Spitfire's basic shape, draw a rectangle with a circle inside and add lines to represent the wings and tail.

Step 2. Next, sketch the outline of the wings, body and tail around the guidelines, and add wheels.

Step 3. Add more detail, including a large circle around the body to suggest the propeller in motion. Then go over your pencil outline in black pen.

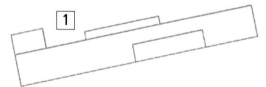

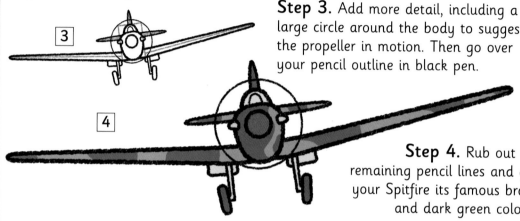

Step 4. Rub out any remaining pencil lines and give your Spitfire its famous brown and dark green colours.

Side-on View

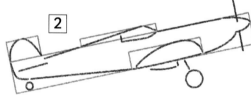

Step 1. Start by sketching a long rectangle, followed by three smaller rectangles.

Step 2. Draw the outline of the Spitfire inside the guideline boxes, and begin to add details such as wheels and a propeller.

Step 3. Continue to add detail, including the markings. Then go over your outline in black pen.

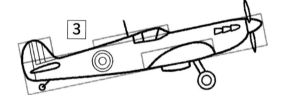

Step 4. Rub out the guidelines and colour in your Spitfire, giving it a green and brown camouflage pattern.

Flying Fortress

Are you brave enough to take on this mighty Flying Fortress?

Fact File

The Flying Fortress was a heavy bomber flown by the British and Americans in World War Two.

Angled View

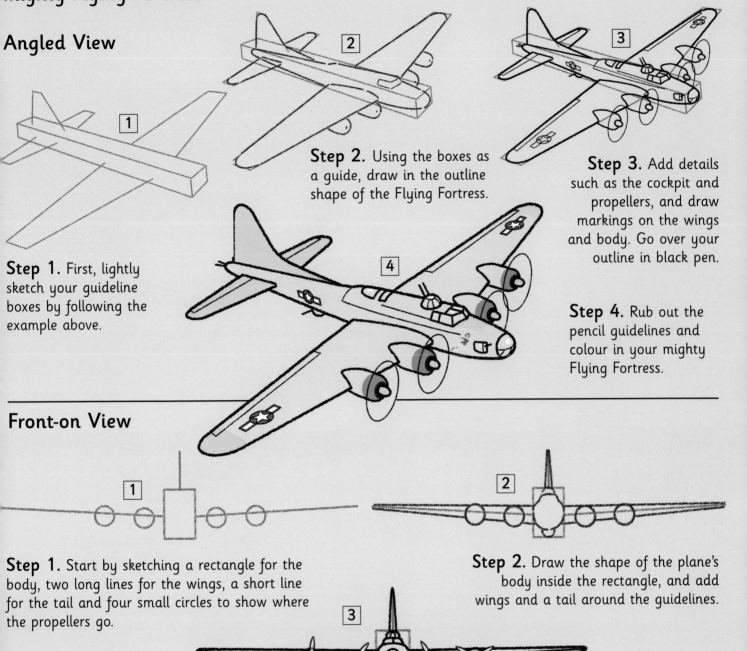

Step 1. First, lightly sketch your guideline boxes by following the example above.

Step 2. Using the boxes as a guide, draw in the outline shape of the Flying Fortress.

Step 3. Add details such as the cockpit and propellers, and draw markings on the wings and body. Go over your outline in black pen.

Step 4. Rub out the pencil guidelines and colour in your mighty Flying Fortress.

Front-on View

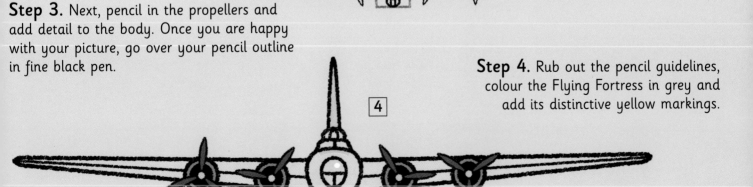

Step 1. Start by sketching a rectangle for the body, two long lines for the wings, a short line for the tail and four small circles to show where the propellers go.

Step 2. Draw the shape of the plane's body inside the rectangle, and add wings and a tail around the guidelines.

Step 3. Next, pencil in the propellers and add detail to the body. Once you are happy with your picture, go over your pencil outline in fine black pen.

Step 4. Rub out the pencil guidelines, colour the Flying Fortress in grey and add its distinctive yellow markings.

Eurofighter Typhoon

The streamlined Eurofighter Typhoon is based on a triangle shape.

Fact File

The Eurofighter Typhoon has a very aerodynamic shape, meaning the air flows around it easily, allowing it to travel very fast through the sky.

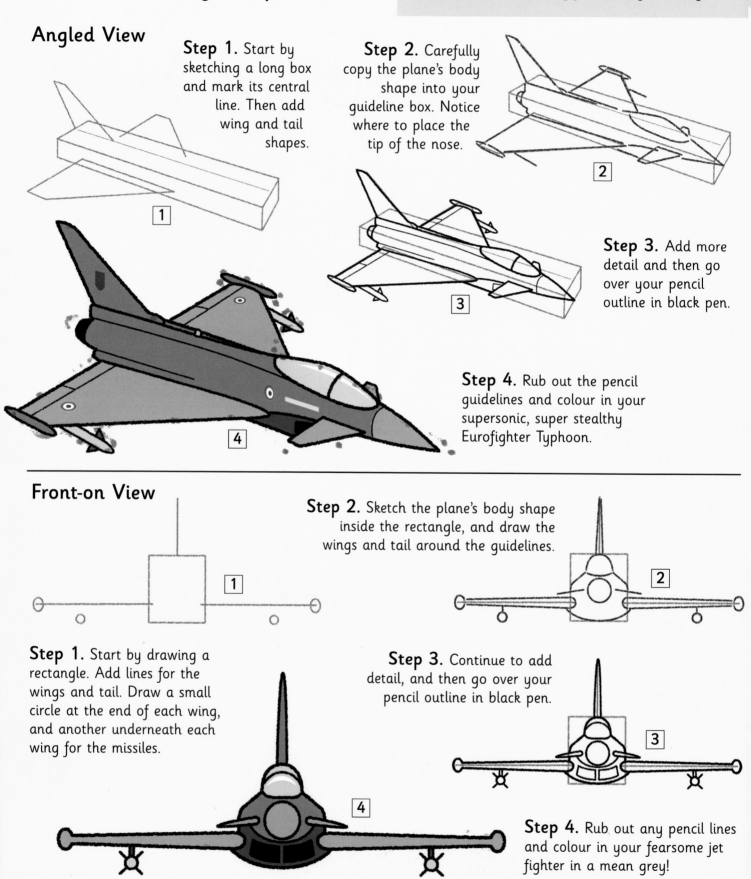

Angled View

Step 1. Start by sketching a long box and mark its central line. Then add wing and tail shapes.

Step 2. Carefully copy the plane's body shape into your guideline box. Notice where to place the tip of the nose.

Step 3. Add more detail and then go over your pencil outline in black pen.

Step 4. Rub out the pencil guidelines and colour in your supersonic, super stealthy Eurofighter Typhoon.

Front-on View

Step 1. Start by drawing a rectangle. Add lines for the wings and tail. Draw a small circle at the end of each wing, and another underneath each wing for the missiles.

Step 2. Sketch the plane's body shape inside the rectangle, and draw the wings and tail around the guidelines.

Step 3. Continue to add detail, and then go over your pencil outline in black pen.

Step 4. Rub out any pencil lines and colour in your fearsome jet fighter in a mean grey!

Boeing 747

Fly away to a distant land in this fantastic Boeing 747!

Fact File
The Boeing 747 is sometimes referred to as a 'Jumbo Jet' or 'Queen of the Skies'.

Front-on View

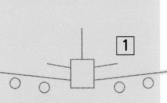

Step 1. For your guidelines you'll need a rectangle, five lines and four circles.

Step 2. Next, build up the shape of your large, heavy plane around the guidelines.

Step 3. Add details such as the window, nose cone and engines. Then go over your pencil lines in black pen.

Step 4. Rub out any remaining guidelines and colour in your fabulous Boeing 747 passenger plane.

Angled View

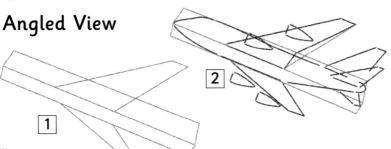

Step 1. Start by drawing a long box to represent the body. Half way along, add two wing shapes.

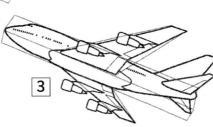

Step 2. Draw the outline of the body inside your guideline box. Then add the tail and engines.

Step 3. Build up the detail, adding flaps and windows. Now go over your outline in black pen.

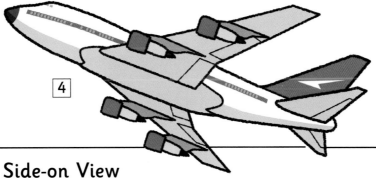

Step 4. Finally, rub out any remaining pencil lines and colour in your plane. You could even create a colourful design for the tail fin!

Side-on View

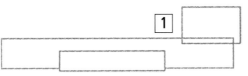

Step 1. Using a pencil and ruler, draw a long rectangle for the body, then two smaller ones to show the position of the wings and tail.

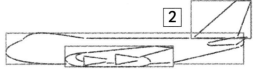

Step 2. Next, draw the outline of the plane inside your guideline boxes, following the example above.

Step 3. Add windows and the front part of the engines. Once you are happy with the picture, go over your outline in black pen.

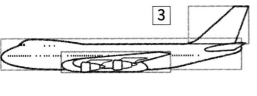

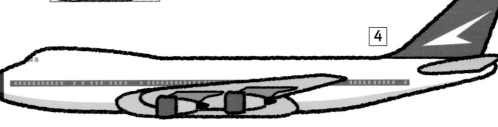

Step 4. Rub out the pencil guidelines and colour in your Boeing 747. Don't forget to give it an eye-catching tail design!

Conclusion

The more you practise, the easier your drawing will become.

Now that you have drawn all of the pictures in this book, why not have a go at doing some stunning drawings of your own?

Choose a vehicle and spend time looking at it before you begin. Try to see it in your mind as a series of basic shapes. Study its proportions and angles.

Top Tip!

Remember to look closely at the basic shapes and how they relate to each other in size and shape. This is the key to successful drawing!

Perhaps the most important thing to remember is to always draw what you can actually see, not what you think something looks like!

Now take out your sketch pad, pencils, a sharpener, an eraser and a pen – **and get drawing!**

Drawing Cartoons

You can have great fun using your new drawing skills to create cartoon vehicles!

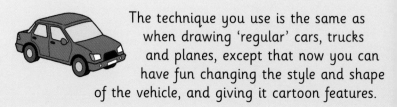

The technique you use is the same as when drawing 'regular' cars, trucks and planes, except that now you can have fun changing the style and shape of the vehicle, and giving it cartoon features.

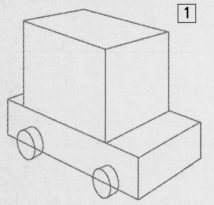

Step 1. Sketch a thin box for the lower part of the car's body, and two cylinders for wheels. For the fun top half of your cartoon car, sketch a tall box.

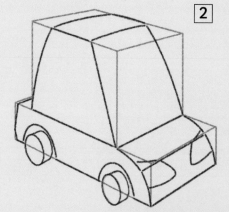

Step 2. Next, draw the car's outline. A very short bonnet makes the tall top half of the car look funnier.

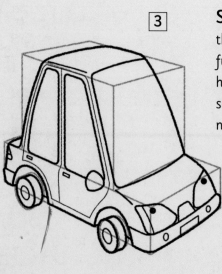

Step 3. As well as distorting the car's shape, you can have fun changing its features. Large headlights look like eyes, and a small radiator looks like a nose! Work up the detail and go over your outline in pen.

Step 4. Finally, rub out the pencil guidelines and colour in your cheeky cartoon car.